RACE AND FREE SPEECH

RACE AND FREE SPEECH

Violating the Taboo

Ray Honeyford

The Claridge Press
St Albans

First published in Great Britain 1992

by The Claridge Press
27 Windridge Close
St Albans
Herts
AL3 4JP

Printed by
Short Run Press
Exeter, Devon

ISBN 1-870626-23-0

Honeyford, Ray: *Race and Free Speech: Violating the Taboo*

1. Politics

CONTENTS

The Personal Context

It would be tempting to use this occasion to excoriate all those anti-racist zealots who, for the past eight years or so, have done their level best to make my life a misery. I would not be short of instances.

I recall, for example, that misbegotten alliance between Islamic fundamentalists and left wing manipulators which led to my early retirement from the headship of a school in Bradford. I still have vivid memories of misguided Muslim adults forcing nine year old innocents to hold up placards proclaiming my fascist intentions; and of the same people waving aloft skull and cross-bone banners besmirching my family name for the delectation of millions of television viewers.

I remember, too, more recent insults administered at some of our universities. There was the time I needed a heavy police bodyguard to bash my way into King's College, London, afterwards being pursued down Fleet Street by a megaphone-wielding mob. There was the successful attempt by a group of bawling left wing bully boys to prevent my black supporter and me from participating in a debate at thc London School of Economics — an institution famous for its commitment to intellectual freedom. I remember being cornered and my life threatened at Lime Street station by two thugs from Liverpool University. I recall the large group of police officers and private security men needed to get me into and out of Hull University. I remember the sickening shock I felt when a heavy metal container was thrown at my head at Sheffield University. At Bristol University it required a front bench of husky rugby players to protect me from a bunch of raging student ideologues -- who marked my departure by throwing paint at me. And I recall sitting in the taxi afterwards with spit running down my clothing. I recall in short the irrational hatreds provoked by someone who wishes to address race relations issues, but who is not prepared to accept the standard anti-racist explanations and rhetoric. Worst of all, I continue to experience a sense of shock and betrayal that so many of those charged with running our universities are unable or unwilling to defend the one thing, above all else, universities stand or fall by — free speech.

Not all the opposition I have encountered has come from student hot heads, political pterodactyls and Muslim zealots. Far from it. Statements about me of a hostile and damaging nature by apparently respectable bodies have become a not uncommon part of my daily experience. Bradford Council, the BBC, and the Commission for Racial Equality have all been responsible for utterances highly injurious to my good name. As I write, I receive notification that the prestigious journal *Educational Studies* is to carry profuse apologies in its next issue in connection with an outrageously inaccurate and defamatory article it had previously carried.

It would, indeed, not be difficult to make this pamphlet into an excuse for settling old scores. But that is not my intention. I have no bitterness about the past. Many others have had to endure far more than my petty discomforts in order to defend free speech on this issue. Moreover, I can balance the negative against the positive. For instance, I have very happy memories of my visits to the Oxford, Cambridge and Durham Unions, where I was treated with great courtesy — not least by those who did not share my views. The same can be said of the universities of Keele and Kent. And, to offset the hostility I have met in some quarters, I am comforted by the considerable support I continue to receive from people of goodwill from all walks of life, and from across the political spectrum.

I come not to moan, but to warn. My experiences are the tip of an iceberg. The threat to free speech on any issue involving race is a very real one, and one which affects not only the general intellectual climate, but the lexicon of private discourse itself. Only certain prescribed perceptions and opinions are permitted. Challenging the viewpoint and the vocabulary of the race relations lobby and its supporters can be a hazardous enterprise. Combining honest dissent with the notion of goodwill to all men — however decent one's intentions, however free of racialist sentiments one may be — is virtually impossible. This denial of a basic right, which we in this country take for granted, not only violates something deep in the national experience, it creates the sort of frustration which generates offensive comments in the tabloid press, produces a mood of dismay in the well-meaning majority, and provides the racial bigot with ammunition. It is, in my view, the greatest single threat to good race relations in this country. If the price we have to pay for our transformation into a multi-racial population — in a sense unique in our history — is a serious denial of free speech, then that is a price which, ultimately, the British public may not be prepared to pay. We cannot begin to confront the real issues, unless and until there is much greater openness in the climate of opinion surrounding the whole issue of race. The present oppressive and dishonest climate is a prescription for race relations failure.

We in this country ought to be heeding the warning which is being beamed loud and clear across the Atlantic. The American dream has been shattered. The melting pot which created the most successful immigrant nation in history is no more. The USA today is a nation sundered by factional infighting and ethnic conflict. This is due, in no small measure, to the failure of the Americans to maintain free speech on an issue vital to its future as a coherent nation. Like us, the Americans have allowed the terms of the debate to be prescribed by guilt-ridden liberals, radical zealots and race relations professionals.

The following opinion is based on American observations. But it could just as appropriately apply to the situation in this country.

> In matters of race there is no such thing as free discussion. There are obligatory pieties, suppressed questions and cancerous duplicities.... Thought controllers have become so much a fact of life as to be not only unopposed, but almost unmentioned.[1]

These are not, as some would undoubtedly allege, the ramblings of some rural red neck, with a chip on his shoulder about race. They are, in fact, the considered opinion of the distinguished American authority on ethnic minority issues, Professor Thomas Sowell -- whose life began in poverty-stricken Harlem, and whose ancestors were African slaves.

Why the Problem?

The factors which, in this country, conspire to create and maintain the bizarre climate surrounding the subject of race are many and various. Orwell's comment in his essay, "Notes on Nationalism", suggests one source: "Within the intelligentsia a decisive and mildly hostile attitude towards Britain is more or less compulsory."[2] The presence in this country of very large numbers of people who are the product of colonialism has undoubtedly hardened this anti-British attitude, and helped to give it an even more malign influence on our national fortunes. The other influences may be characterised as liberal guilt, historical associations, left-wing opportunism, and bureaucratic self-interest.

The advent of large scale immigration from Britain's former empire provided those of liberal disposition with a field day. Here, indeed, was the occasion for that grand humanitarian gesture which well-meaning liberals need to assuage their consciences about all those wrongs the Empire is alleged to have perpetrated. Attacking that hostility with which all newcomers in any society are invariably faced, liberals were able to parade their virtuous intentions, whilst calling for ever-increasing state intervention in race relations, so as to abolish prejudice and discrimination — a policy more likely to exacerbate than to solve the problem. In point of fact, this well-meaning but muddled liberal response has been decisive in creating that state-controlled race relations apparatus which has done so much damage to free speech.

But, to be fair, it is not only those who have allowed their hearts to rule their heads who are afflicted by guilt when considering any issue involving race. We are all, to some extent conscience-stricken. We need to acknowledge this, before we can begin to establish an attitude which is at once rational and humane. We need, that is, to grasp the extent to which race is associated with negative historical images. We all, inescapably, link race with practices, events and institutions which are appalling in their human insensitivity and monumental wickedness. We are all heirs to feelings of repugnance and shame when considering what men have done in the name of race. We are all haunted by images of rejection, cruelty and hatred. The horrors of the Atlantic slave trade have been instilled in our minds since childhood. Apartheid, though less pitiless than slavery, is, nevertheless, synonymous with the denial of the most basic of human rights, with suppression of legitimate aspirations, and with cruelty. And there is the violation of all that makes us human summed up in the word "Holocaust". We can never forget that the greatest crime in history was carried out in the name of race. Is it any wonder, then, that race is a taboo subject, something we prefer not to approach, let alone honestly to confront and discuss? Or that such an explosive subject, capable of generating enormous emotional energy and revulsion, should be exploited by those with an ideological axe to grind? After all, the major problem for those whose aim is radical, root and branch changes in the social and political order is to create an enthusiastic following. There is always a need for dramatic issues to sustain the faithful. What more sensational cause could there be than race, with its vivid and appalling historical reverberations?

Both the sectarian left and the racialist right know this. And both have sought to exploit to their advantage the unprecedented changes in the racial make up of Britain's population, which have occurred over the last forty years or so. However, there is a distinct difference in the impact political extremists have had on the debate about race in this country in recent decades. The fanatical right, whose propaganda connects so readily with all the guilt-inducing images we have discussed above, continues in the social and political wilderness. It is despised by the respectable citizen, plagued by relentless internecine conflict, and fails lamentably to enlist the popular vote. Conversely, the militant left has had considerable success in exploiting the race issue. Its depiction of Britain as a "racist society" has struck a nerve in the liberal conscience. At the same time the left has successfully managed to link racial conflict with the essential but flagging thrust of the class struggle — a development which has sustained sectarian ardour. There is no doubt that the political left has had great success in laying down the terms in which race issues are to be discussed; and the principal component in the anti-racist ideology created by the left is white guilt.

But the left has done more than dictate the terms of the debate. It has dominated policy-making in this area. The notion that human values and relationships should be subject to state control -- a central tenet of sectarian left-wing theorising -- has been largely conceded. Increasing intervention by politicians in race relations is now the order of the day. There are a number of reasons for this. The militant left is well represented in those local authorities controlled by the Labour Party; it can count on significant support within the Parliamentary Labour Party; and the left's relentless stress on the importance of capturing the ethnic vote has struck an echo in the minds of all those politicians representing multi-racial constituencies -- whatever their political allegiance. That is, the sectarian left, unlike its right-wing equivalent, has been, and continues to be, the decisive political influence in matters to do with race. Moreover, the left's political advantage has been echoed in the academies by a group of left-wing intellectuals who have hammered out a view of Britain's racial character, which, though seriously one sided, has been enormously influential, not least in the state education service.

Perhaps the best illustration of how the left successfully allied the notion of white guilt about race with the imperatives of the class struggle was the determination of the Inner London Education Authority to impose on its schools and colleges the all-embracing theory and practice of minority politics. The association of race with the class struggle was unashamedly proclaimed. The pedagogical inanities of "multi-cultural education", and the moral idiocies of "anti-racist education", were imposed on schools and colleges, and teachers dissented at their peril.

This mentality is firmly embedded in the Labour Party's most recent policy document *Opportunity Britain*. Although this document is vague, ambiguous and generally confused about social issues, it nevertheless makes clear that the accession of another Socialist government will be marked by a considerable increase in political coercion in matters to do with race.

There will be a new and tougher Race Equality Act. There will be "ethnic monitoring in employment, housing and other services" -- with the inevitable corollary that inequality of outcomes will be used to justify quota systems. Contract compliance, which demands that firms working for the government must establish racial quotas, will in due course, "be extended throughout the public service". There will be a new legal process for dealing with race cases, and channelled through "Equality Tribunals" -- and these will be empowered to pay out "increased compensation". Moreover, unrepresentative lobby groups will be enabled to bring cases of a collective nature.

In short, the next Socialist government will seek to impose on the citizen the notion that there is a "politically correct" view of matters to do with race, and this will enter into every aspect of our social and economic life. The fact that this sort of state intervention has been a disaster in the USA, where it has been in existence for several years, will do nothing to deter the social engineers from seeking to impose politically-defined virtuous behaviour on their fellow men. Race politics is now a significant feature of the designer socialism created to fill the vacuum left by the discredited "class struggle".

The political phenomenon has its bureaucratic counterpart in what is popularly known as "the race relations industry". This functions at both the official and voluntary level. At the latter level there is no doubt that there exists a genuinely humane concern for the welfare and progress of the ethnic minorities -- as at the Runnymede Trust; (although there are voluntary organisations whose aims are indubitably ideological, eg, The Institute for Race Relations). At the official level there are the countless Race Equality Councils (formerly Community Relations Councils): a group of assorted race experts employed by local authorities and government departments, and, pre-eminently, The Commission for Racial Equality, a statutory body with considerable legal powers. These various bodies are united by their view of race relations, and of the condition and progress of the ethnic minorities in Britain. They are all committed to a negative outlook about the state of race relations, and all have a striking tendency to depict the minorities as a universally failing and exploited under-class. Britain, in their view, is rotted with endemic "racism". And there is need for an unrelenting struggle to cleanse our society of this all-pervading pathology. The considerable success of many ethnic minority groups, and the generally tranquil state of race relations -- these things, which are obvious to the impartial citizen, form no part of the rhetoric of the race-relations lobby. This is not surprising, particularly in those whose career prospects depend on the discovery, cataloguing and publicising of every instance of "racism" -- real or imagined -- which exists. The race lobby's unrelenting pessimism helps to make the vital public debate about race that we need to conduct virtually impossible. Its manifest lack of balance not only affronts the majority population; it reinforces that disabling guilt which plays a key role in preventing genuine free speech.

Even worse, this relentless, institutionalised pessimism about ethnic possibilities reinforces a sense of hopelessness among some young, inner city blacks. It helps to put chips on their shoulders. By being constantly urged to blame "the system" -- rather than honestly to face the issue of personal failings and inappropriate group values -- young blacks are increasingly inclined to take refuge in resentment and displaced anger. Thus, the solution appears to be, not courageous self-help to overcome the undoubted prejudice which exists, but anti-social behaviour. The very people and institutions ostensibly concerned with harmony and integration, therefore, are, ironically, increasing the possibility of misunderstanding, resentment, and perhaps even conflict. A better prescription for producing bad race relations, and for halting ethnic minority progress could scarcely be imagined.

The race issue, then, functions in a climate of bad faith. Guilt, political and bureaucratic vested interest, and the sneering anti-patriotic attitude of large sections of the chattering and scribbling classes these things conspire to prevent the sort of intellectual freedom we take for granted in other areas.

Does Race Exist?

To the vast majority of people this will appear a foolish and unnecessary question. Indeed to many biologists, anthropologists and psychologists, too, it would appear redundant. Nevertheless it does need to be raised, if only because immensely influential voices, well known for their attempts to supply the anti-racist lobby with some sort of theoretical respectability, argue either that race does not exist, or, if it does, that it has absolutely no significance. Such an attitude, of course, functions to restrict free and open enquiry and discussion. If a human condition does not exist, or is of no value in understanding human problems, why raise the matter in the first place? Moreover, there is a strong suggestion in the anti-racist literature, that scientists who insist that race does exist and ought to be investigated are themselves covert racists -- a charge so serious that only the brave are prepared to pursue the matter.

Yet both dictionary and the most recent text-book proclaim the reality of race -- which suggests a strong supposition in favour of its existence. Moreover, both dictionary and text book insist that race is a biological concept. A recent, standard text book in psychology says this, "the clearest, although still quite complex, way to consider race is biologically. In practice, it seems best to start with the definition that a race is a reproductive community sharing a common gene pool. This definition applies to the human population as a whole: and thus different races are sub-groups.... Thus it is certainly possible to distinguish between races on purely biological grounds, without considering cultural factors."[3] The standard text, *Races of Man*, states, "Man is a polytypic species, that is, one consisting of several subspecies and races." The 1991 issue of the Encyclopaedia Britannica defines race as follows: "biolgical grouping within the human species, distinguished or classigied according to genetically transmitted differences" (p. 876)[4] There are few specialists, it seems, who would want to question this obvious truth, though some might want to distinguish between genetic and geographical sources. Only those who regard science from a strongly held ideological position would want to dissent. Yet it is this latter group who dominate the debate.

Nor are the dissenters to be dismissed as eccentrics, comparable to flat-earth theorists, or advocates of phrenology. Far from it. Some are well-meaning academics holding chairs in English universities. Thus John Rex, the leading anti-racist theoretician, and adviser to the immensely influential Swann Committee, who holds the chair of "Ethnic Relations" at Aston, argues that biology has nothing to contribute to the study of race. Race, he holds, is a purely social phenomenon understood, not through decades of scientific enquiry, but by the investigation of social conditioning. The corollary of this view appears to be that, if people were conditioned in a different way, or, to use the sociological jargon, if we were to "deconstruct the obvious", then race would effectively disappear.[5]

A team from the Open University, headed by Stephen Rose, professor of biology there, appear to agree with this. "In biological terms," they write, "the concept of race is meaningless for human populations." Strangely, in the same paper, we find the following: "For the biologist "race" is a technical term, which may apply to all species. A race is a variety of a species within which there is a free exchange of genes (the unit of heredity) by interbreeding and which may be distinguished from other varieties by some common and heritable attribute."[6] Unless we deny that humankind is a "species", it is difficult to see how these mutually exclusive statements can be reconciled. On the one hand we are told that race is biologically meaningless, whilst on the other we are informed that race exists and can provide knowledge of how to categorise sub-species, one of which, presumably, is *homo sapiens*.

This denial of race as applied to the biology of people is a standard characteristic of the literature of the anti-racist movement. It is as though race is too awkward a notion to subsume within the accepted ideological, view of things. Rejection of the obvious, refusal to confront such a transparent aspect of reality, may arise from a number of sources. It may arise from the guilt which is so strongly associated with race historically; or it may arise from the cast of mind which insists on an ideological blueprint in terms of which all life's mysteries can be explained. Concepts which disturb this sort of reductionism, however scientifically well founded they may be, have to be rejected if the blueprint is to remain intact and valid. The cognitive dissonance which results from countervailing information then becomes too painful to accept.

This rigidity has two consequences. First, there is a desperate attempt to rationalise the offending concept by constructing an alternative, all-purpose, explanation; in this case by rejecting the proven existence of race as a biological concept, and relying wholly on cultural and environmental notions. Secondly, there is a relapse into an authoritarian attitude towards those who insist upon the validity of the established concept, and on their right to investigate relevant phenomena. Both these attitudes can be seen at work throughout the literature created by those who perceive society as a simple conflict between the evils of racism and the virtues of campaigning anti-racism. It is no accident that the founding fathers of the anti-racist ideology are all on the far left — Fanon, Mullard, Sarup, Sivanandon are all committed to a Marxist position. Marxists, of course, are pre-eminently prisoners of their own world view, and have given massive evidence that, where this conflicts with reality, then it is reality rather than theory that must be re-constructed.

As we shall see, this mentality has had disastrous consequences for the spirit of free enquiry. It has helped to make race a taboo subject, to be approached -- if at all -- only by those armed with the approved anti-racist credentials. To insist upon the biological reality of race is to risk consignment to those nether regions thought to be inhabited only by fascists and Nazis. Worst of all, the ideological view of race risks the creation of a consensus science — of the kind we associate with the infamous name of Lysenko.

Is Britain a "Racist Society"?

Those who argue that race is, essentially, a false and misleading myth are, oddly enough, often the self-same people who insist that all white people are racists, and also that only white people can be guilty of this offence. In other words, though race does not exist, racism has a definite racial basis; it is determined by one's racial group membership. This strange lack of consistency in no way disturbs the mental tranquillity of those who insist on exclusive white guilt. Far from it. The same people not only impugn individuals who have the misfortune to have been born the wrong colour, they insist that the whole of our society is afflicted by the same virulent disease. The allegation that contemporary Britain is a conspiracy against racial minority groups is the central conviction of the whole anti-racist lobby. The Commission for Racial Equality -- either directly, or by implication — ceaselessly conveys this message to the media through press releases, surveys, reports and proposals to the Home Secretary. Countless Race Equality Councils hammer the same message home at the local level. Social science course throughout the country seek to persuade students that racism is endemic, not merely at the individual and societal level, but in the deep, unconscious levels of the collective mind. That idea is a bedrock assumption in teacher-training. So successful has the accusation been that the BBC relentlessly, and as a matter of course, transmits the message as gospel truth; it has even established a special unit called "Mosaic", which, to judge from the programmes so far transmitted, has the single aim of convincing all of us that to reject or even question the notion is evidence either of stupidity or covert racism.

This same BBC outfit has an "Education Officer" -- one Mr Europe Singh — who in January 1991 put on a BBC-sponsored conference entitled "Race Equality Education and Training for the 1990's". This portentous gathering brought together the great and the good from the whole race-relations hierarchy, in order to consider ways and means of converting those dissenters, back-sliders and eccentrics who perversely insist upon questioning the allegation that we can be legitimately described as a racist society.

It is no exaggeration to say that this deeply offensive allegation has attained the status of a revealed truth. It is self-evident and not to be questioned. So pervasive is its influence that, in certain walks of life, to suggest it may be false is to risk one's career. So powerful are those who come bearing this message, and so insistent their propaganda, that one never sees the charge seriously challenged. Every discussion about race relations and the fortunes of the ethnic minorities in this country has to begin by the participants implicitly accepting that the anti-racist lobby's depiction of our society is valid.

But truth is not a function of the amount of support an idea can enlist. We live in an age in which people's understanding of reality is often the product, not of honest truth-seeking, but of insistent propaganda. Moreover, people have prior reason to accept as true whatever protects their own interests -- and the vested interests involved in maintaining this particular conviction are considerable. Anti-racism is not just an idea or theory. It is a lucrative career-structure with powerful political aspects.

It is important to bear in mind that when anyone alleges that Britain is a racist society, he is not simply pointing to the obvious truism that some people are hostile to minority groups -- that is true of every society, whatever the perceptual signalling involved. He is asserting that we are, as a matter of public policy and private reaction, a nation committed either explicitly (as with the immigration laws), or implicitly to racial discrimination. And the only effective answer to the problem is to follow the sanitising policies helpfully provided by the anti-racist establishment: positive action, reverse discrimination, contract compliance, numerical targets in the labour and housing markets, and the imposition of a multi-cultural curriculum and an anti-racist policy in our schools. Only thus, it seems, can we be cleansed of the corrupting influences of our inherited bigotry. Only thus can we achieve the ultimate objective of racial equality -- where equality means equality of outcome.

If we are to ensure that real free speech exists on this issue, we need first to examine whether this underlying assumption is valid. Is it true, or is it a distortion of reality? Are our immigration laws influenced by racial considerations? And are the variations in socio-economic outcomes the results of a systematic and malign conspiracy against blacks and Asians, or are they, rather, the result of our living in a free society, in which variations are inevitable?

It is certainly true that our immigration laws are designed so as to reduce the inflow from the Indian sub-continent and the Caribbean. And to that extent they can be validly seen as taking skin colour into account. Rightly or wrongly, politicians of all parties — when in power -- feel compelled to reflect public anxiety and take race into account in seeking to control immigration. But to argue that this proves racial hostility *per se* is to oversimplify what is a complex decision: a decision, moreover, which was not made at the outset of large scale, post-war immigration. For no less than fourteen years (1948-1962) this country pursued an open door policy, and made entry freely available to every Commonwealth citizen, whatever the colour of his skin. That could not have happened if the people of this country were significantly concerned about the question of race -- the politicians would in that case never have permitted an open door policy for any length of time. The policy of successively restricting entry was not the result of knee-jerk prejudice. It was a function of experience. The country as a whole began to realise that skin colour was highly correlated with considerable variations in culture, particularly in the peoples of the Indian sub-continent. There were enormous differences in languages, religions and general cultural outlooks. Perceptions of West Indians were soured by a series of riots, which, whatever the favoured explanation, caused considerable public alarm. Moreover, it came to be realised that successfully integrating peoples of different races into the fabric of society was much more difficult than doing so with our traditional caucasian immigrants. If you are black or coloured in an overwhelmingly white society, then your difference from the majority is emphasized and dramatised. Hence acceptance is likely to take longer, and you are, deplorably, but inescapably, more likely to encounter intolerance. In short, the British came to accept the inescapable truth that creating and maintaining a successful multi-racial society was much more difficult than they had ever imagined. Restrictive immigration was a realistic acceptance of this fact, rather than a racially-inspired policy. Moreover, a series of statutes conferred special legal protection on ethnic minorities and gave them exclusive access to certain public funds -- so that those who were here were more likely to feel welcome. Control of immigration came to be understood as a necessary aspect of good race relations.

It is true that disadvantage is not randomly distributed. The Policy Studies Institute survey of 1984 showed that on key socio-economic criteria blacks and Asians did fare worse than whites when the whole country was considered. However, when the data were controlled for location, and analysed in relation to inner London, Birmingham and Manchester, the variations disappeared. Ethnic minorities were no more likely to be poor and underprivileged than the local majority population. As the Oxford sociologist S J D Green has recently suggested, this points not to racial discrimination, but to a factor of general urban disadvantage from which all inner city inhabitants suffer.[7]

Moreover, there is growing evidence that cultural -- not racial -- variables are playing an important role in determining outcomes. For instance, we now know for certain, that despite the fact that they are treated no differently at school, Asian pupils do far better, on the average, than West Indian pupils in public examinations. Indeed, in the age range 16-24 Asian youngsters are not only doing better than blacks in acquiring skills and in penetrating further and higher education. They are also outperforming their white counterparts. These results cannot begin to be explained by the thesis that our society is endemically racist. They inescapably point to cultural influences. Whether the anti-racists like it or not, different ethnic groups *do* espouse different value systems, and these are manifestly correlated with degrees of success in life. For instance, it could be that Asians are so dramatically out-performing West Indian groups because they are the products of more stable and secure family backgrounds; a factor which may well help to explain why certain Asian groups are beginning to do better than their white school mates, who also tend increasingly to come from broken homes.

Unless and until these sorts of important cultural factors are allowed to enter the analysis, then no one is entitled to ascribe socio-economic variations to racism. But in the present repressive climate reference to such factors is likely to elicit accusations of racist intentions.

Again, the anti-racist lobby not only insists upon the exclusive influence of racial discrimination in explaining social and economic outcomes; it also constantly asserts that inequality of outcome proves inequality of opportunity. If proportionately fewer members of the ethnic minorities are enjoying the fruits of life, this establishes beyond question the fact that they are being denied equal opportunities with whites. This is transparently dubious.

In the first place is it not to be expected that historically recent immigrants and their immediate descendants will, for obvious cultural reasons -- language being one of them -- tend to lag behind the indigenous population for a considerable time? Secondly, if we argue that variations in outcome are *per se* malign, and that equality of outcome is always desirable, then that is a political stance, as applicable to social class as to race. The political left has always argued along those lines — the attainment of equality and the abolition of human variation are the hallmark of socialist societies, not of free societies such as ours. Variations of outcome are not, in free societies, the exception. They are the norm. The truth is that people, faced with the same opportunities in life, make systematically different choices, both at the individual level and at the group level. This is bound to mean a patchwork of outcomes, rather than a neat, statistical pattern with proportionate class and racial representations.

Moreover, in our kind of society institutions such as the labour market are not, in any sense, democratic. We do not appoint or promote people on the basis of a franchise, as we do our politicians.

Workers do not "represent" anyone. They are simply hired to carry out a specific function on the basis of individual merit. Since different groups in society espouse different values, and have different aspirations, we should expect variations in socio-economic outcomes to occur. And such, indeed, is the case. But this proves, not that we are a racist society, but a free one.

The principle is amply illustrated in those areas where the ethnic minorities outperform the majority population. Asians, for instance, do better than the majority population in terms of home ownership — a key indicator of socio-economic success. We have already noted disproportionate Asian success in education. Blacks are massively "over-represented" in prestigious, big-time sport: at the last Olympic games our black athletes comprised one third of those chosen, when the target population was probably no more than two or three per cent of the population. Yet no one complained that this was evidence of discrimination against white competitors.

Again, if the allegation of endemic racism is to convince, then we need to resort to international comparisons. And does anyone seriously suggest that this country's treatment of its minorities can begin to compare with the positive savagery we observe in both the African and Arab worlds, not to speak of the atrocious treatment of the Chinese populations in south Asia? As Russell Lewis has reminded us, Muslims are far safer in Bradford than in Indian Kashmir, or, indeed, parts of France. A Tamil is better protected in Twickenham than in Sri Lanka; a Sikh is more at home in Southall than in New Delhi. A Chinese person has a better chance of advancement in any part of this country than in Malaysia, which operates anti-Chinese quota systems. And a black person is far more secure in Cardiff or Liverpool than in northern India.[8]

It is worth asking, too, why it is that overtly racist groups in this country never obtain any more than derisory electoral support, unlike their counterparts in, say, France, Belgium, Italy, Germany, Japan and the USA. Moreover, if we are as the anti-racist lobby depicts us, why is it that this country is a Mecca for people of every race, creed, and colour from every part of the globe? Could this continue to be the case, if racial hostility and discrimination were rampant?

Sociological attempts to establish how far the British people are racially prejudiced have ended in confusion. So highly charged is the subject of race, so hedged about with ideological and bureaucratic interests, that attempts to provide statistically evidence have ended in fierce and acrimonious quarrelling between the contending parties. Professor Marten Shipman has reviewed the evidence in *The Limitations of Social Research*. His conclusion provides no comfort for the anti-racists: "The result of the ensuing debate over the status of the evidence leaves the problem of the level of racial prejudice in Britain as open as ever."[9]

However, we might get nearer the truth if, instead of beginning with an accusation, we began with a question, namely: "What is a racist society?" History provides, by common consent, three examples — the southern states of the USA before the civil rights legislation, Nazi Germany in the 1930's, and apartheid South Africa. These were very different societies. But they all had certain things in common. They all allocated civil rights on the basis of supposed racial characteristics. The state, echoing and reinforcing society's attitudes and beliefs, used three devices to maintain the dominant race's superiority: the continuous propagation of a theory of racial supremacy and inferiority; a legal and educational apparatus which implemented the theory and transmitted it to future generations; and political procedures for enacting, and police and military organisations for enforcing, the appropriate legislation.

If we define a racist society in this historically verifiable way, rather than on the basis of an anti-racist conspiracy theory, then, clearly, this country does not qualify. We do not underpin our institutions with any odious racial theory; we do not relate civil liberties to skin colour; and we do not regulate access to the welfare state according to ethnic origin. On the contrary, as far as the state is concerned, Britain positively favours its minorities, in terms both of protective legislation and exclusive public funding.

It is instructive in this context to consider the opinion of someone who eventually became a vice-chairman of the Commission for

Racial Equality -- Professor Bikhu Parekh: "I did not at all wish to suggest that Britain is a racist society, nor that every Briton is a racist. Such a suggestion would be utterly false and grossly unfair. When all is said and done, Britain is one of the most decent and civilised societies in the world, and is characterised by a considerable sense of fairness and humanity." (*Five Views of Multi-racial Britain*, CRE, 1978).

That being so, one wonders why the organisation to which, for so long, Professor Parekh was attached, spends so much of its time, energy and public money in seeking to maintain that the very reverse is true -- and helping, thereby, to maintain the debilitating bad faith which surrounds this issue.

This relentless insistence on the truth of a manifestly questionable myth does more than violate the normal rules of honest discourse. It generates entirely understandable resentment in those — the vast majority -- who stand falsely accused of this grave moral delinquency. Worst of all, it provides those who are racists with the opportunity of exploiting this resentment. Thus the anti-racists not only outrage the decent majority; they provide their ostensible opponents with campaigning sustenance. It becomes that much easier for the ideologues of the extreme right to disseminate their notions of white supremacy. One outrageous myth thereby begets another.

The Double Standard

Denial of free speech is bad enough. But when free speech is being differentially determined -- and on the basis of race -- that adds insult to injury. It would be difficult to do more to generate racial tension than by allocating free speech on the basis of racial group membership. Yet this is precisely what appears to have happened. I have spoken on this subject in many parts of this country, and to a very wide range of audiences -- and wherever I go (with the exception of certain university audiences) I am confronted with this same issue: why is the majority population denied a freedom which members of the ethnic minority clearly enjoy? I was, initially, very much inclined to treat this sentiment with a good deal of scepticism: the result of a vague sense of disquiet, perhaps, about our recent transformations. But I no longer believe that. There does appear to be a considerable imbalance. Examples abound.

Take the matter of incitement. A foolish and angry white person in Cheltenham makes an offensive remark about a black parliamentary candidate, and is immediately summoned before the magistrates to answer for his misdemeanour — to the undisguised delight of the whole anti-racist establishment, no doubt. Yet the founding fathers of anti-racist ideology in this country have produced a literature rampant with vicious, anti-white sentiments. Consider this, taken from a seminal text in the anti-racist canon:

> All the time I was writing *Black Britain*, I found not solace, comfort or tolerance, but tension, a disturbing desire to break, smash and riot, to bellow: "Whitey, one day you'll have to pay".... Already we have started to rebel, to kick out against our jailers.... The battle will be a bloody one.... Blacks will fight with pressure, leaflets, campaigns, demonstrations, fists and a scorching resentment which, when peaceful

> means fail, will explode into street fighting, urban guerrilla warfare, looting, burning and rioting.... To these I say, "Watch out, Whitey, Nigger goin' to get you."[10]

The writer of these words is black. He was not required to answer to the authorities for his incendiary rhetoric. On the contrary. He flourished in the authoritarian culture of radical sociology, and was rewarded with a chair in one of our most famous universities.

Again, consider the Rushdie case. Certain Asian Muslims not only burned books — triumphantly, and as a carefully stage managed television event to be seen by millions. They shouted highly provocative slogans, burned Rushdie in effigy, and carried banners which appeared to incite, not simply to hatred, but to murder. And one of their leaders uttered words in public which were transmitted to every home in the land via television news bulletins, and which, in the view of all independent observers, including the broad sheets, constituted a very serious offence indeed. The authorities denied there was sufficient evidence to justify a prosecution, and the individual concerned got off scot free.

It is instructive, too, to consider that, whilst *The Satanic Verses* has been removed from certain public library shelves, or is available only from under the counter, anti-Christian literature written by Muslims is readily available -- not least in Bradford, the focal point of Muslim protests, as a correspondent to the *Bradford Telegraph and Argus* has pointed out.[11] For instance, *Islam, the Natural Way*, was published in 1989, a year after the Rushdie book appeared, and in the same year as the book burnings began. The author of this book describes the Bible as, "unfit to be regarded as scripture". Christianity he condemns as "inadequate as a world view", the Trinity is a "monstrous" concept, the Resurrection is firmly rejected, Christ's divinity is" an awesome blasphemy", and the reader is informed that "the Bible is not the word of God". This crude anti-Christian tract, written by an educated British/Asian Muslim, would be very likely to give deep offence to a devout Christian, yet it, and many like it, are freely — and quite properly -- available in our libraries and book shops.

The same duplicity is apparent in the publicity surrounding a speech delivered to a private meeting by John Townend, MP, who uttered these words:

> When Muslims say they cannot live in a country where Salman Rushdie is free to express his views, they should be told they have the answer in their own hands -- go back whence you came.[12]

This was immediately condemned in several journals, a Labour MP raised the matter in Parliament, and there were calls from anti-racist activists for Mr Townend's prosecution.

However, some time before this, a Dr Shabbir Akhtar wrote a defence of fundamentalism in *The Guardian*. Dr Akhtar is a Muslim, Bradford-born and educated in this country and Canada; he is a leading member of the Bradford Council of Mosques, and a professional race relations official. Dr Akhtar wrote these words:

> Those Muslims who find it intolerable to live in a United Kingdom contaminated with the Rushdie virus, need to consider seriously the Islamic alternatives of emigration (*ijrah*) to the House of Islam, or a declaration of Holy War (*jehad*) on the House of Rejection.[13]

This was met with a resounding silence. No one protested. No one even whispered the possibility of the authorities being involved.

Yet whilst Dr Akhtar clearly agreed with Mr Townend about the possibility of re-location, he went very much further. He not only suggested departure as a solution, he pointed the way to the most violent of solutions to the problems of inter-group conflict — Holy War.

In a recent issue of the journal *Literary Review*,[14] the distinguished writer V S Naipaul, who is a Trinidadian of Indian descent, advocated precisely the same solution as that put forward by Mr Townend, but in considerably stronger language. But, again, there was no suggestion of protests from any quarter. Skin colour, it seems, is operating on this subject to create differing notions of intellectual freedom.

The extent to which this double standard is thought, in certain influential quarters, to be acceptable can be judged from the incident described by Professor Michael Banton in his book *Promoting Racial Harmony*. This illustrates that the mentality I am describing is not confined to the over-heated rhetoric of anti-racist agitprop, and the nervous ambiguities of officialese. It is a way of thinking to be found at the very heart of academe itself. Professor Banton quotes one of his black colleagues as saying that "No black scholar should ever criticise any other black scholar in public." That is, if you are black, you are functioning in a climate free of the normal, rigorous demands of truth-seeking. This racist sentiment could only have been uttered in a society in which matters to do with race are surrounded by double thinking and hypocrisy.

Race and Education

The anti-racist movement has had great success in the field of education, both in terms of what happens in schools and colleges, and in the area of research which has implications for education. Children, young people and teachers are being given a view of matters associated with race and race relations which is often seriously inadequate. And those who seek the truth about such matters in a dispassionate, scientific manner, free of ideological bias, are often the object of harassment and personal and professional obloquy.

The relationship between language and race, for instance,is often wrongly presented. Words such as "nationality", "ethnicity" and "culture" are, quite wrongly, taken to be synonymous with the word "race". The word "black" is grotesquely assumed to be applicable to all non-white people -- a verbal sleight of hand which not only robs distinctive cultural groups of their unique identity, but actually gives offence, not least to our many and diverse Asian groups. More than that, this perverted use of the word "black" carries with it the real and dangerous possibility that the world ought to be seen in terms of black solidarity versus white intransigence. Is it any wonder that so many of our youngsters -- white as well as black -- finish up with a chip on their shoulders about race, when exposed to this sort of distortion?

Again, take one of the favourite words in the anti-racist lexicon: "stereotyping". This word originates in the field of social psychology, and refers to a process taken to be involved in inter-personal perception. We all, it is claimed, have a tendency to judge other people and groups by generalising on the basis of one or two dominant features, and so oversimplify and often distort our impressions and judgements. The concept may have some validity, when used in this strictly limited way. But in anti-racist discourse it is invariably applied to any negative judgement made about any ethnic minority individual or group, so as to discredit that judgement; however well founded it may be. The result is that white people are afraid of making any critical statement, for fear of being accused of the insensitive attitude that this word connotes. The minorities are deprived of honest feedback, and relationships are falsified.

Our language itself is charged with being deeply and incontrovertibly "racist". English, our young people are daily informed, is a covert conspiracy against black people. References to "black" in the language, some of which have negative connotations, are references to black people. This, pupils are told, is an inevitable consequence of certain historical developments, the chief of which is colonialism. Black people are therefore bound to be negatively perceived by white people, because the language used by white people is imbued with a traditional hostility to blacks.

This crude linguistic determinism has been shown by scholars in this country and the USA to be deeply flawed. Studies of the history of words and phrases involved, word-counts of negative and positive associations, and comparisons of English with other languages -- not least those used by black nations -- have indicated that this thesis is highly dubious.[15] Yet this does not prevent impressionable young people from being regularly told that it is both valid and indispensable to an understanding of race relations.

Again, consider the sort of texts which are in regular use in our schools. One example will make the point. In 1988 the distinguished publishing house of W & R Chambers issued a school book entitled *Multicultural Britain.* This purported to be a full and rounded picture of our race relations, and of the position of the ethnic minorities in contemporary Britain. To those of us familiar with the methods and assumptions of the anti-racist lobby, the implicit purpose would appear to be to convince pupils that this country is a society rotted with endemic, guilt-inducing racism. The whole thing is permeated with a tone of unrelieved pessimism and despair.

The ethnic minorities are shown as being the victims of more or less systematic discrimination, and doomed to failure, while the many instances of ethnic success -- not least the Asian success in education

-- are totally ignored. Immigration laws are not, according to the authors, a rational attempt to cope with the many cultural and race relations problems unrestricted entry inevitably brings. Nor are they a response to well founded public anxieties. They are simply an indication of racial hostility. The English language is, predictably, accused of being "racist". The notion that race even exists is dismissed as "a false belief". The British Empire is disposed of as having been concerned entirely with exploitation. Complex phenomena such as housing, wage levels and race riots are presented in grotesquely over-simplified terms. All the ethnic minorities are labelled "black" — and all the important variations within them thereby suppressed. References to Nazi genocide and South African apartheid sit beside an illustration of racist graffiti in English.

Middle class people are presented as materialistic, smug and grasping; working class people as resentful, downtrodden and deprived. There are lots of carefully selected quotes, and a great deal of bubble language appears. Not surprisingly there are no quotations from one, Karl Marx, whose incendiary, anti-black rhetoric would have landed him in gaol, had he been expressing his view in this country today.

In short, this is little more than anti-racist rhetoric, with a rather crude left-wing subtext, carefully packaged to be digested by immature pupils, whose parents expect teachers to present both sides of the story when dealing with controversial issues. How are the pupils to know that the authors' view of the sociology of race in this country is grossly oversimplified, highly tendentious and unjustifiably pessimistic? The fact that this book was quickly re-printed suggests that a significant number of teachers were persuaded to buy it, and use it in the classroom -- presumably because they agreed with the picture it presents; or, perhaps more likely, because they were too hard pressed with their teaching duties to give the thing the properly critical reading it demands.

The treatment of those who claim to have established a link between IQ and race, again, illustrates the extent of successful anti-racist activity in the field of education. I have no wish to take sides in this highly charged and acrimonious debate. I simply wish to point out the consistently intolerant atmosphere in which it is being played out. Those who claim to have established a link between race and intelligence are not merely held to be mistaken. They are also accused of being wicked. Jensen, Shockley, Eysenck and others have all been traduced in print and harassed in person. The most recent victim of this kind of abuse is the Canadian Professor Jean Philippe Rushton. Rushton is a distinguished researcher who for decades has been studying human variation. He claims that it is possible to distinguish differences according to race, including variations in IQ. Since Rushton announced his results in 1989 the following things have occurred. A former prime minister of Ontario called for his dismissal. He was linked with Nazism, the Ku Klux Klan and Anti-Christ in a variety of journals and speeches. The Ontario police launched an investigation of Professor Rushton, demanded tapes of his lectures, and sent a long questionnaire to his lawyer. The Attorney General of Ontario denounced him as a "loony". And his employers, the University of Western Ontario, gave a critical report on his performance as an academic, and threatened his tenure.[16] This spectacular display of intellectual bigotry occurred, of course, because Rushton's insistence on the right of a scientist to pursue the truth -- wherever that might lead him -- violated the prevailing taboo. The only research acceptable to the anti-racist establishment is the sort which prefigures no link between I Q and race.

Even to consider the possibility that race might be a factor in explaining variations in academic performance is not a permitted attitude in polite society. In every age something is taboo. In ours that something is race. Any research which includes reference to race is automatically suspect. Positive results are not acceptable to the prevailing orthodoxy, and individuals who challenge that orthodoxy are bound to suffer. The Galileo syndrome did not end with the Middle Ages. It is alive and well in our age. If the influence of race as a factor in educability could be scientifically established, that fact would be as inconvenient for received opinion today as was Galileo's cosmic discovery to the establishment of his day. This sort of anathema leads in one inevitable direction "consensus science", i.e., science conceived, not as truth seeking but as self-serving mythology.

The late Beverly Halstead, reader in geology at Reading University, provided a clear exposition of the political background to this controversy.[17] A powerful scientific lobby dominated by the radical left has come to dictate the subject, and to prescribe the terms of the debate. The Radical Science Movement in the USA, and the British Society for Social Responsibility in Science have insisted that, because the outcome of research into race could be abused by those with an axe to grind, such research should not be permitted. This is like insisting that, because Hitler claimed his preposterous theories of racial superiority derived from Darwin, then we must suppress the theory of evolution. According to Dr Halstead this lobby, or at least the mentality it reflects, has succeeded in bringing about the closure of an important department of the Natural History Museum. This department formed a world-wide centre for physical and biological research and the study of human variations. Its life was hastily and mysteriously brought to a close in 1985 -- a dramatic decision which officialdom has, it seems, never pretended to explain or defend. An important educational resource was thereby lost -- probably for ever.

The nature of the prevailing intolerance and the way it influences received opinion in education is clear from a pamphlet issued by the Open University in 1978. *Race, Education, Intelligence—A Teacher's Guide to the Facts and Issues* was commissioned and distributed by the National Union of Teachers (NUT). The NUT is the biggest of the teacher unions, and in 1978 it had a much larger membership than it has now. It is no exaggeration to say that the leadership of the NUT is often regarded by the public and the media as the authentic voice of the whole teaching profession. Its influence on public opinion would be difficult to overstate. Equally, its influence in forming the views of the rising generation through its members' teaching activities must be enormously important.

Every member of the NUT received a copy of the NUT pamphlet. And there is little doubt that most would have accepted its views as unchallengeable. The imprimatur of the Open University and the

NUT general secretary would have given it an infallible status in the eyes of teachers. Its influence has been enormous. It has been quoted *ad nauseam* in the literature of the anti-racist lobby. It is regarded as the seminal guide in the environmentalist corpus.

Yet this pamphlet is a very questionable statement in relation to the subject it purports to address. The authors not only deny that there are demonstrated average differences in intelligence according to race; they appear to deny that race exists in a biological sense at all. They reject the notion that intelligence can be measured, and attack both IQ tests, and those psychologists who believe in them. They ascribe interest in this area to "Scientific Darwinism", drop broad hints that the whole enterprise is really about establishing the notion of white superiority, and use the term "scientific racism" to identify work in the field. An implicit link is made with the National Front. And the authors conclude by questioning the integrity of those they oppose: "We must, therefore, seriously question the intention of those who persist in asking this question and attempt to give it scientific status." In plain, honest English do not the weasel words "seriously question" mean that they consider the intentions of their intellectual opponents to be morally suspect?

Now much of this can be dismissed as extreme egalitarian cant. What is inexcusable is that such an enormously influential document should be so one-sided. For instance, the racial differences in intelligence discovered by psychologists are dismissed as "supposed": the implication being that such differences do not actually exist. Yet every standard text book published over the last forty years or so states that they do exist. A standard text in psychology for A level and undergraduate studies published just two years after the pamphlet was issued, drawing on evidence from as early as the 1920's and confirmed by work as recently completed as the 1970's, says this: "In general, it must be accepted that the difference (with regard to race and intelligence) is a consistent one, and not due to accident or error."[18] Of course the reasons why such differences occur is a matter of legitimate and continuing debate. What is inexcusable is that a group of academics, writing for such a huge and influential audience, should seek to dismiss scientifically established fact.

Even worse is the tone of this unfortunate pamphlet. Throughout there is a strong suggestion that the investigation of racial differences is motivated by a desire to prove white racial superiority. This outrageous slur has gained considerable credence, not least in both teacher-training and the classroom. Yet it is patently untrue. Psychologists working in this field, eg, Professor Richard Flynn, have consistently pointed out that whites do not do best on IQ tests. Orientals are always superior to whites. Moreover, many reported studies have pointed to the intellectual superiorities of Jews. These are, indeed, strange and perverse findings on the part of people motivated by a belief in white supremacy. However, of all the evidence for the suppression of the truth in any matter linked with race — however tenuously -- the fate of a piece of vital research commissioned by the Swann Committee is, perhaps, the most dramatic.

The Swann Committee of Inquiry into the education of ethnic minority children spent nearly £700,000 of public money, took nearly six years to complete, and produced a report 807 pages long.[19] It had the resources both to carry out surveys of existing knowledge and to commission original research. The key question the committee confronted was this: Why is it that children of West Indian origin do less well, on the average, than not only white, but also Asian, children viewed collectively? There had been consistent and continuing allegations from the anti-racist lobby that the explanation lay in racist teachers purveying an essentially white-dominated curriculum. This thesis had received some support from the preceding Rampton Report, though no remotely convincing evidence had been adduced to confirm it.[20]

In order to examine this issue the committee engaged a leading educational researcher, Dr Peter Mortimer, then chief of research with the Inner London Education Authority -- an organisation noted for its support for anti-racist theorising and practice. A contract was signed, a teacher seconded as research assistant, and a grant of £78,000 allocated for the work to be carried out. The proposals for the research included an investigation into "the factors in school, in the community, and in the home that led to success or failure of ethnic minority pupils". This key purpose was based on the terms of reference of the Swann Committee, recommended in the interim Rampton Report, and supported by the firmly established and universally accepted belief that children's progress in school — whatever their race — is powerfully influenced by the school, the community, and, crucially, the home. Rampton had actually stated: "We intend to look at this whole question of home background in respect of ethnic minority children in our main report." Moreover, Swann had explicitly accepted that in considering this issue the general culture and family environment of West Indian pupils were crucial factors: "The reasons for the very different performances of Asians and West Indians seem likely to lie deep in their respective cultures... the tight-knit nature of the Asian community and family -- more so than whites and Indians -- could explain the differences (in achievement rates) since parental influences on educational success have long been recognised."

In addition the researcher was to look -- and with particular care — at the background of successful West Indian pupils, so that lessons could be learnt which would be of benefit to the whole West Indian community. The basic purpose, in other words, was constructive.

When the research proposal was made known, however, there was intense opposition. The source of this opposition has never been revealed. Whether it came from those race-relations professionals on the committee who supported the explanation in terms of "white racism", from certain anti-racist organisations operating in the state education service, or from the source Samir Shah has described as "the ideological boot boys of the race relations industry", we shall never know. Whatever the source of the opposition, it was successful. The research was suppressed. (Lord Swann himself used the word "abandoned".) The reasons for the opposition are obvious. If Dr Mortimer's work had gone ahead it might well have produced evidence that the anti-racist explanations of comparative black failure were bunkum. That would have dealt a serious blow to the political and professional vested interests which such explanations help to sustain. The myth of racism in the classroom had to be maintained.

Lord Swann in commenting on this episode said the committee was left "with little chance of deciding with certainty the relative importance of the many factors in the educational system and outside it, that might be, or are held to be, crucial."[21] In other words, the central purpose for which the committee had been formed -- and in pursuit of which it had spent over half a million pounds of public money -- was frustrated. Because the pursuit of truth by disinterested research was not permitted, we knew no more about why West Indian children perform comparatively badly in school at the end of six years of deliberations than we knew at the first meeting of the committee.

If there is a lesson to be learnt from the Swann fiasco it is surely this: unless the forces of truth are willing and able to take on and defeat the huge vested interests of the race-relations industry, then we can never produce an atmosphere conducive to genuine and honest race relations in education — or in any other area.

The authoritarian mentality I have been seeking to illustrate has had a disastrous effect on the culture of the state education service. Absurd curriculum theories abound, genuine moral education is perverted, relationships are falsified, and charlatans are regarded as experts. It has never been more necessary for us to face the issues associated with race; and it has never been more difficult, thanks to the triumph of falsehood.

Race and the Law

The bad faith surrounding the issue of race has created academic intolerance, ideological conflict and a self interested bureaucracy. But it has done more than that. It has helped to establish laws, which, far from encouraging understanding and harmony, have actually generated confusion and resentment.

In the misguided, and essentially ideological, debate about what principles should underlie the enactment of laws -- the classical liberalism which stresses equality under the law, the importance of individual liberty, and the right to private property; or the notion of "rights", as in the right to work and the right not to be discriminated against -- there is no doubt that the latter doctrine has won out in those areas where the law concerns itself with race. The successive Race Relations Acts of 1965, 1968 and 1976 have systematically and with increasing rigour sought to weaken established liberal principles, and substitute the notion that the law must be tilted in the direction of state intervention to ensure that the ethnic minorities are granted certain supposed rights to equality of outcome in the fields of work, housing, education and public institutions generally. The notion that racism is uniquely evil and requires unprecedented legal regulations and constraints to control it has been officially endorsed. The citizen experiencing any form of discrimination or hostility arising from his ethnic identity is, we are told, in a uniquely heinous position.

But is this so? Racism is certainly morally repugnant. For people to be denied opportunities, or to be subjected to social rejection, or even actual hostility, on the wholly irrelevant grounds of skin colour -- that is clearly barbarous. No civilised human being would tolerate it. That is not at issue.

But is it the case that evil customs and crimes motivated by race are intrinsically more reprehensible than those arising from other causes?

On what basis should we judge the seriousness of these things? Is it more diabolical to refuse someone a job or promotion on grounds of religion or class, than on grounds of race? Is it more wicked to assault someone on the grounds that he is a different race from you, than on grounds of, say, political differences? To put the matter another way, if I hit a man on the head with an iron bar because he is black, and I hate black people, is that a more serious offence than if I do the same to another man of my own race in order to steal his purse? The criterion is surely not the motive involved, which can always be denied, but the perpetrator's basic intention and the degree of injury caused to the victim. It is the intrinsic nature of the offence which counts. Yet we have laws on the statute book which make race a special and uniquely important human attribute. Moreover, categorisation by race is only ever applied to those of minority skin colour. It is held to be irrelevant for the majority. It is difficult to see how this can be equated with the principle of all citizens being equal under the law, or with the admirable objective of good race relations.

Race is also held to be uniquely significant in the matter of free speech. Incitement to racial hatred -- though not to political, religious, or class hatred -- has been given a privileged position in law. Yet powerful and wholly adequate restrictions on free speech already existed before the race laws were enacted. Defamation, sedition, national security and public order — all these were the objects of legal regulation and restriction.

Moreover, the race laws introduced a rare and dangerous principle, namely that intention does not have to be established for conviction to occur. A new offence, that is, was accompanied by the violation of a fundamental principle of law — that in order to prove a particular offence has been committed, *mens rea* has to be established beyond reasonable doubt. The vital principle of intention was swept away in the Race Relations Act 1976. Many leading jurists deplored this. Professor Harry Street, in the standard text, *Freedom, the Individual and the Law*, says, "the need for this new offence is questioned" -- there being ample powers under the existing Public Order Acts. Professor Street goes on to say this: "The cause of legal control of discrimination is only harmed by Parliament imposing criminal sanctions which give others the opportunity to whip up frenzy among those who are easy victims of crude propaganda.... The right of freedom of expression must be jealously safeguarded." "Whipping up frenzy" about matters of race has, of course been the fell purpose of the sectarian left over the past thirty years or so. This deplorable Act has, inter alia, allowed aggressive ideologues at some universities to curtail free speech for visiting speakers, by systematically and deliberately mixing up the principle of free speech with the issue of public order.

But not only did the matter of race issue in a law which created a new offence, and abolish the vital principle of *mens rea*, it also created a law which is logically and obviously flawed in principle. This is so in two respects. The relevant section of the Act uses the phrase "threatening, abusive or insulting" to describe the speech or writing which might stir up racial hatred. Now a court could, conceivably, seek to objectify "threats", or — less securely — the notion of "abuse". But how is the term "insult" to be given any sort of meaningful status? People may take offence on very trivial occasions. Some people have a very low flashpoint. Since the necessity to prove intention is now abolished in this context, it is not difficult to see how this constitutes a threat to free speech.

Secondly, as Roderick Moore has pointed out,[22] why should it be an offence to incite people to do something which is not, in itself, an offence? Hating someone, or a group of people, may be morally deplorable. But it is not a violation of the law. If it were, then we should all be up in court at some point in our lives. It makes good sense to prohibit incitement to commit assault, rape, murder, because they cause death or human suffering. But does it make any sense to prohibit a desire to incite anything as deplorably commonplace as hatred? If it does, then why are not other forms of incitement to hatred banned? Left wing organisations — the most vociferous supporters of the mentality underlying the race-relations laws — constantly seek to provoke class hatred. Why is that not a criminal offence?

Bad laws have unfortunate consequences. By reinforcing and

surrounding with the majesty of the law the understandable anxiety people feel about race, parliament has powerfully influenced the climate of opinion -- a climate of opinion in which decent citizens are afraid to express legitimate anxieties. Charlatans can flourish, their propaganda unchallenged, precisely because people are afraid they might be in trouble with the law if they express contrary opinions. The incantation "racist" is often not a word honestly denoting a fact, but a weapon wielded by zealots in order to suppress dissent. It is often uttered as though it were a synonym for "rapist" or "fascist". It is applied to anyone who dares to disagree with the anti-racist consensus. "Racist" has, in truth, become the rallying cry of some of the most intolerant elements in our society. Half-truths, misrepresentations, and downright lies about race relations and the actual condition of the ethnic minorities have come to be accepted as self-evident truths, because that vigorous public debate, which is the only effective safeguard against falsehood, has never taken place. This lacuna has been caused, in large measure, by profoundly unwise legislation.

The mentality which produced, and has sought to maintain and strengthen, the race relations acts has been adopted, developed and refined by the Commission for Racial Equality (CRE). Its submission to the Home Secretary, *Review of the Race Relations Act 1976: Proposals for Change*, is a chilling commentary on the position we have reached. The intolerant intentions of the CRE are there revealed for all to see. Increased restrictions in the field of advertising — which already labours under severe prohibitions — are the least of the massively increased powers the CRE is demanding. The necessity to establish a racial motive in cases of alleged indirect racial discrimination would be abolished. The assumption of pre-verdict innocence would be swept away — to be replaced by a presumption of guilt, with the burden on the defendant to prove otherwise. The irrational and dangerous principle that inequality of outcome is proof of racial discrimination would be formally enshrined in law. The notions of "disparate impact" and "historic disadvantage" — which have had a disastrous influence on race relations in the USA — would become an essential part of race-relations theory, and used as weapons in the courts. Racial quota systems — though not to be described as such -- would be effective in every walk of life. The necessity to produce *prima facie* evidence of discrimination — as established in the famous *Prestige* case -- before the launching of a racial investigation would be swept away, and the CRE empowered to carry out rigorous investigations on mere suspicion. A new "Tribunal of Fact" would be created to sidetrack the usual judicial procedures. The CRE would supervise immigration controls, and "all areas of governmental and regulatory activity" -- including planning, the prisons, and the police. The CRE would also acquire powers to interfere directly in the administration of education, without reference to the Secretary of State. In short the CRE would be assigned powers of accusation and investigation unprecedented in our history. Without undue exaggeration the CRE's ambitions have been compared with those of the Spanish Inquisition. A development more likely to intensify the ill-will and bad faith surrounding the whole issue of race in our society would be difficult to imagine.

In *Anti-Racism: A Mania Exposed* Russell Lewis has spelled out just how far the existing bad faith has produced anti-racist censorship in journalism, television, libraries and publishing. In the media, for instance, a militant group at the National Union of Journalists has imposed on its members a code of conduct which effectively seeks to prevent any adverse comments about any person or organisation belonging to the ethnic minorities.[23] The CRE has directly sought to influence the reporting of racial matters on television in a special report *Television in a Multi-Racial Society.* The initiative appears to have led to the creation of the unique anti-racist unit at the BBC, known as "Mosaic". As I have said, this outfit, to judge from the programmes it transmits, has the sole purpose of convincing the British public that we are a "racist society". Organisations such as "Librarians against Racism and Fascism", and "Librarians for Social Change" have made it clear that libraries exist, not for the usual reasons, but to spread the anti-racist gospel. Here is a typical sentiment expressed by the former: "We, as librarians, agree it is a major function of librarianship actively to combat racism and fascism, and we advocate the following: that stock selection for libraries should be guided by anti-racist and anti-fascist principles. That staff selection should reflect a similar policy", i.e., librarians must have the right sort of political opinions. It would be tempting to dismiss this offensive nonsense as the hot air of ineffective extremism. But that would be a mistake.

This mentality, in fact, has had considerable influence, particularly in certain left-wing local authorities, not least in their education services. This offence to civilised values could be illustrated *ad nauseam*. But it is best brought out by the fate, in many areas, of that great classic of American literature *Huckleberry Finn*. There have been attempts to ban it or, perhaps even worse, to bowdlerise it. Not even the fact that the book's hero is the entirely admirable slave, Jim; nor the fact that all the book's villains are white — not even these saving graces are sufficient to save it from the inquisitors.

This urge to trim and shape civilised discourse to the imperatives of the race lobby, and to ban where thought necessary, does not merely outrage those who espouse decent values and truly educated sentiments. It provides the real bigots with ammunition. And it is intrinsic to the way in which our society is being led to react to racial issues.

Race and Crime

A dramatic illustration of this is our response to the link between race and crime. There has been a systematic and relentless attempt to sweep this issue under the carpet — unless the victims belong to the ethnic minorities. The radicalised National Association of Probation Officers expresses alarm at the disproportionate number of blacks on remand, and implicitly condemns the criminal justice system as "racist". The Home Office sets up a special and unique unit to report on "racial attacks". And our magistrates are required for the first time in our history to categorise defendants according to skin colour -- the unspoken assumption being that they are sending down too many blacks, and had better take greater care in future. Yet there is no countervailing concern about the possibility that young blacks might be disproportionately involved as perpetrators of crime. Indeed, there appears to be evidence that the authorities have tried to suppress the data. This is particularly so of crime in London, where much the biggest black population is to be found.

When, in 1983, the Metropolitan Police issued figures clearly indicating the level of Afro-Caribbean crime, there was uproar from certain quarters. The whole anti-racist lobby rose up and excoriated the police as "racists" for daring to reveal the figures. The CRE expressed its strong disapproval. And Mr Roy Hattersley — whose continued parliamentary career depends entirely on his ability to attract the ethnic vote — condemned the evidence as "statistical garbage". Yet the first Home Office survey of ethnic groups in prison in 1986 strikingly confirmed the police view. On average there were ten times as many Afro-Caribbeans as a proportion of the prison population as there were whites. Black males comprise 1% of the general population, but 8% of the prison population, the corresponding figures for black females being 2% and 12%. Moreover, many of the black offences were more serious in a proportionate sense. Nearly 50% of blacks over twenty one convicted of sexual offences were guilty of rape, compared with 14% of whites in the same category.

The anti-racist lobby has always argued that these ethnic variations with regard to crime are a function of racial discrimination and unreliable statistics. Such rationalisation has received consistent support from certain academics working in the field of ethnic criminology. This subject is dominated by Marxists, for whom crime is the result, not of individual moral decisions, but of capitalist oppression. The answer lies in reforming "the system", not in punishing the guilty. But there are brave souls in the most unlikely places. Young and Lea, in *What is to be Done about Law and Order?*, were honest enough to conclude, that, though some police officers are undoubtedly prejudiced, ".... there was a real rise in crime among the West Indian population, and the police, in responding to it, were not responding to a figment of their imagination."

Moreover, though blacks are "over-represented" in crime, Asians, it seems, are "under-represented". It seems rather odd that a system alleged to be infected with racism should discriminate against one ethnic group and not another.

The most recent exposure of this problem came in a House of Lords debate on crimes of violence on 15th March 1989. Lord Reay had this to say:

> Let me give some statistics. In figures released last week by the Home Office (*Statistical Bulletin*, issue 5/89, table 5) covering the Metropolitan Police District -- where, let it be remembered, 60% of all robberies in the country take place -- of those arrested for street robbery in 1987, 61% were black and 34% white. Another table, table B, shows that 85% of the blacks arrested were aged under 21.

(At this point Lord Reay is interrupted by the Bishop of Manchester, but then resumes.)

> Table 5 of the Bulletin also gives figures for all robberies in the Metropolitan Police District. The ethnic breakdown for those arrested is as follows: in 1985, 50% black, ,and 45% white. In 1986, 49% black, 43% white. In 1987, 54% black, 41% white....
>
> As regards Underground robbery, figures were made available to me

by British Transport Police.... In 1987, white 10%, black 80%, mixed race gangs 8%. In 1988, white 10%, black 70%, mixed 19%.

The recent Home Office Research Study 106, *Concerns About Rape*, in a rare excursion into the subject of the ethnicity of the offenders, analysed the result of two surveys into rape in the two London Boroughs of Islington and Lambeth, which were chosen because they have high levels of recorded rape. In Lambeth, with a black population of 14% of the total population, 72% of rape offenders were reported as black. In Islington, with a black population of 6%, 43% of the offenders were reported as black.

The figures are hardly common currency. They are not published in the newspapers. It has been a forbidden subject. I found the Metropolitan Police were immensely reluctant to discuss crime in terms of race.... I believe that the taboo should be broken. The dis-cussion of race and crime should not have to be conducted either in a whisper, or with Nazi slogans, with nothing in between: for to continue to cloak the subject in silence for political reasons is, for one thing, to confer a sense of immunity on the perpetrators of these violent crimes. To do that is monstrously unfair to those who share those areas where crime is endemic, who have to live in bandit country, who cannot leave and who largely provide the prey for the criminals. It is also to fail in our duty to the vast, law-abiding majority of the black population whose members have that much harder a task in setting their children on a lawful career.[24]

A number of points are justified. First, it is difficult to deny that, in the face of this sort of detailed, sober analysis of information from independent sources, there is clearly a serious problem of black crime — at least in London. Secondly, Lord Reay's reference to a "forbidden subject" is obviously, and deplorably, true. Thirdly, the denial of honest feedback to the target community is particularly cruel — no community can give of its best if it is not being allowed to look in the mirror, since the necessary societal pressures to conform to the ideal are being distorted and rendered ineffectual. Fourthly, the attitude of the police, though understandable, is clearly misguided — they are, in effect, party to the deception and evasion.

We cannot begin to face this problem unless and until we reject the supposed right of the anti-racist lobby to suppress information which conflicts with its view of ethnic minorities as passive, sinned-against victims. Nor must we go on accepting the facile argument that to reveal negative data about the minorities is to play into the hands of the racial bigots, who will misuse it for their own nefarious purposes. In the long run the truth, however painful, is the only answer to bigotry. For bigotry thrives on attempts to protect its victims from reality. The present official attitude on the one hand serves to support anti-racist mythology and on the other provides racists with ammunition. The bad faith surrounding race is thereby reinforced. It is very doubtful if the necessary reform in attitudes and intellectual climate can take place, so long as the Race Relations Act 1976 remains in its present form.

Conclusion

Only a blind fool would deny that this country has its fair share of racial bigots, or that we have a tiny minority of racist thugs whose behaviour shames us all. To be a Bangladeshi in parts of Tower Hamlets is to be a target for outrageous abuse or worse. On a certain housing estate in Bradford, where the National Front has some influence, to be Asian is to be mocked, insulted and despised. That is shocking to the civilised conscience, and a stain on our national good name.

But the present, official response to our transformation into a multi-racial society is more, rather than less, likely to sustain discrimination. If we are honestly and constructively to confront the issues surrounding race relations, then there needs to be a radical change in the intellectual climate. We cannot hope for harmony and integration by suppressing free speech, and persecuting those who seek to uphold it. In attempting to get rid of one evil by supplanting it with another, we simply beget more evil.

We must certainly acknowledge our sins. But we must also be allowed to celebrate our successes in race relations. We must stop applying a double standard to the behaviour and attitudes of the majority and minority populations — special pleading upsets the moderate majority, and provides bigots with propaganda. We must stop misleading the children in our schools about the true nature of race relations, and the progress of the ethnic minorities in this country. Imperial guilt and ideological opportunism are spectacularly inappropriate foundations for creating enlightenment about these matters. We must accept that race exists. And we must accept that those who wish to research and publish in this area have a right do so — without fear of abuse, harassment, and intimidation.

We have no hope of effecting this change unless we question the role of the state in race relations, and the structures it has created. The parliamentarians have established a deeply flawed and misguided statute which, far from improving race relations, sustains misunderstanding and resentment. The publicly-funded race relations lobby must be abolished, together with its patronising paraphernalia of social and racial engineering — numerical targets, contract compliance, reverse discrimination, racial head-counts, "codes of conduct" and the rest. These measures can only have two predictable consequences — feelings of bitterness in adversely affected white people, and the production of that most depressing and insulting of all the symbols of race relations mischief, the token black. The racial expert must be sent packing. And politicians angling for the ethnic vote must be exposed and castigated.

We must set before young blacks and Asians models, not of pessimism and failure, but of optimism and success. There is no shortage of these. One such is Leon Hawthorne. Mr Hawthorne is the twenty-four year old son of Jamaican immigrants, and his father is a shoemaker. He went to the local comprehensive school, where he gained eight O and three A levels. He then proceeded to Liverpool University where he obtained a good degree. Initially he pursued a successful career in the City, and is now a television researcher and presenter with the BBC. Mr Hawthorne recently published his views in *The Daily Telegraph*:

> The commission for Racial Equality has achieved nothing for black people in this country and it should be abolished. It was set up under the Race Relations Act 1976 with the aim of eliminating racial discrimination and promoting greater racial harmony. In fact, its actions and policies have exacerbated racial problems, and far from doing any good, it has done a great deal of harm.... The CRE has used its time and spent our money encouraging positive discrimination and disseminating multi-culturalism in our schools. Both these things have rightly sponsored an upsurge in white resentment. Why should blacks get special treatment, and why should our schools be given over to brainwashing our children about their subconscious "racist" attitudes when they refer to a "blackboard" or a "blackspot"? This is a petty and pathetic self-indulgence which has created an intolerable climate

> where no white person feels he can comment on race without being labelled a bigot.... Cultural integration and black success stories should be the goal of race policy.[25]

That is an example and a voice we need urgently to respect. If we ignore Mr Hawthorne's message, we can look forward not to racial harmony and integration, but to resentment and conflict.

REFERENCES

1. Thomas Sowell, quoted in Campus Report, University of Ontario, 1990.
2. George Orwell, "Notes on Nationalism", *The Penguin Essays of George Orwell*, Penguin Books, 1984.
3. J. Radford & G. Govier (Eds.) "A Textbook of Psychology", Sheldon Press, 1980, Second Impression 1982.
4. Sonia Cole, "Races of Man", British Museum, 1965, 2nd Ed. Reprinted 1968.
5. John Rex, "Race Relations in Sociological Theory", Weidenfeld & Nicholson, 1970.
6. "Race, Education and Intelligence: A Teacher's Guide to the Facts and Issues", National Union of Teachers, 1978.
7. S.J.D. Green, letter in *London Review of Books*, 21.4.1988.
8. Russell Lewis, "Anti-Racism — A Mania Exposed", Quartet Books, 1988.
9. Marten Shipman, "The Limitations of Social Research", 2nd Ed. 1981, 3rd impression 1985.
10. Chris Mullard, "Black Britain", Allen & Unwin, London 1973.
11. Rodney Fletcher, *Bradford Telegraph and Argus*.
12. *The Yorkshire Post*, 28.8.1989.
13. *The Guardian*, 27.2.1989.
14. *Literary Review*, October 1990.
15. Linda Hall, "Language, Race and Colour", in "Anti-Racism — An Assault on Education and Value", Sherwood Press, 1986.
16. *The Times*, 10.6.1991.
17. *The Salisbury Review*, Vol. 5, No.2, January 1987.
18. J. Radford & G. Govier (Eds.), see above.
19. Lord Swann, "Education for All", Cmnd 9453, H.M.S.O., 1985.
20. Anthony Rampton, "West Indian Children in our Schools", Cmnd 8273, 1981.
21. Lord Swann, "Education for All: A Brief Guide to the Main Issues of the Report", H.M.S.O., (1985).
22. Roderick Moore, "Racialism and the Law", Libertarian Alliance, 1986.
23. National Union of Journalists, "Guidelines on Race Reporting", 1987.
24. *Hansard*, 15.3.1989.
25. *The Daily Telegraph*, 20.6.1991.